A Kalmus Classic Edition

Johann Sebastian

BACH

SIX FRENCH SUITES

AND TWO SUITES IN A MINOR AND E♭ MAJOR

Edited by

HANS BISCHOFF

FOR PIANO

CONTENTS

K 03041

Kalmus

PREFACE

Since I am issuing a new edition of the Bach Suites, may I first be permitted to express my gratitude to the libraries and individuals who have provided me with such a wealth of manuscript source-material, the extent of which has, in my opinion, never been available to any previous editor. It is a well-established fact that Bach had made many copies and recopies of his own works; the original form of the composition was frequently altered in these later copies. One can detect signs of the composer's indefatigable desire for improvement in almost all the movements of the French Suites. It is, therefore, not at all surprising to find two or more authentic documents contradicting each other. The intrinsic difficulty in editing lies in the necessity of establishing which of the various versions of a work, or portion of a work, represents Bach's ultimate intention, i.e. which version he would himself have chosen as the one best suited for publication. It is, therefore, exceedingly important to be familiar with the sequence in which various autographs of the same composition were written. Criticism of the text is made increasingly difficult by the fact that some of the corrections contained in a particular manuscript may be traced to an alien handwriting. One can readily perceive the importance of securing the most exhaustive collection of authoritative manuscripts for all the numerous works of Bach which did not appear in print during his own life-time. Conjectural criticism, which cannot be avoided entirely in instances of uncertain tradition, must be based on the exhaustive study of the most thorough source-material. Previously published editions of the French Suites, some of which were doubtless edited with care—(the English Suites have not undergone as many transformations as the French Suites)—all share a common limitation in that they faithfully follow only the one particular document in the possession of the editor. I could even cast a most serious aspersion upon the Bach-Gesellschaft edition, particularly because it has won such monumental acclaim through the work of the highly deserving Dr. W. Rust and other musicological leaders—in that the editing of the Suites by an unnamed person is as ill-befitting as the editing of the Inventions by Mr. C. F. Becker.

We possess the following works of Bach written in suite form: the three well-known collections of the six French Suites, the six English Suites, the six Partitas, the French Partita, a Suite in F major (See Spitta, Vol. 1, Page 428) the Suites in A minor, E flat major, E minor (see Spitta, Vol. 1, Page 768), also a few fragments.

For historical and pedagogical reasons it is best to consider the French Suites first. I believe it is proper, in a critical edition of the Suites, to include the ones in A Minor and E flat major (cited above) together with the group of French Suites—to which they belong not only because of their form, but also because of their appearance in the extremely important collections *C* and *D* (see below). I should like to add, in this connection, that I have no point of vantage from which to determine just when Bach selected the six familiar suites out of the entire group of suites written in the manner common to the French Suites. Nevertheless, I am certain that he did make the selection himself. I must also leave unanswered the question why the suites were called "French." Apropos the English Suites—Forkel states that they were composed for an eminent Englishman.

My manuscript source-material for the French Suites is as follows:

A. The little "Klavierbüchlein" of Anna Magdalena Bach. (Royal Library in Berlin.)

B. The large "Klavierbüchlein" of Anna Magdalena Bach. (Royal Library in Berlin.)

C. The Rust-Wagner copy, derived from Friedmann Bach's legacy. (Royal Library in Berlin.)

Documents *A*, *B* and *C* are actual autographs.

D. Gerber's copies. (Property of Dr. Erich Prieger, Berlin.)

E. A copy of the C minor Suite, spuriously listed in the catalogue as an autograph. (Royal Library in Berlin—P. 274.)

F. A copy of the first E flat major Suite. (Royal Library in Berlin—P. 289.)

G. A fragment of the G major Suite. (Royal Library in Berlin—P. 212.)

H. A copy of the French Suites originally owned by Kirnberger. (Amalien-library #76.)

J. A complete, more recent copy. (Amalien-library #50.)

K. A copy of the second E flat major Suite. (Amalien-library #552.)

The following analysis of the relative authoritativeness of these documents will serve to justify my eclectic procedure in reconstructing the text. It will also serve to prove that a positive decision by the editor in certain instances could only be interpreted as an obviously arbitrary action. I sincerely hope that the performer will be interested in studying the different variants from the authentic manuscripts, so that he can make his own logical choice. Our text contains, to be sure, only thoroughly authenticated versions.

A contains the authoritativeness of an early manuscript. One may deviate from it if a later variant bears the stamp of proven authenticity. The little book, dating from 1722, contains twenty-five pages—not all of them in correct sequence. Fragments of the first three French Suites appear in it; the fourth and fifth Suites are complete. The original sequence appears to have been as follows: the third, fourth and fifth Suites were definitely in correct succession, the one in C minor probably preceded them, a fragment of the D minor Suite probably came at the beginning of the little book. I see no reason for assuming a different sequence for the Suites, particularly since the D minor Suite definitely comes first, and the C minor Suite is called the *second*—in *B*. In *A*, several short pieces are written after the G major Suite. They are of little consequence —excepting three Minuets, one belonging to the C minor Suite, another in B minor subsequently added to the Suite in the same key, and one in G major that was probably intended as a supplement to the G major Suite.

B dates from the year 1725. It contains, in addition to some compositions which we do not have to discuss at this point, the complete D minor Suite and the C minor Suite almost up to the end of the Sarabande. The manuscript contains several free variants; moreover, it is written in a very cursory manner. I counted over thirty careless errors in script.

C is an autograph which was passed on from Friedmann Bach to F. W. Rust, then to Dr. W. Rust. In 1844 the firm of Peters received it for the purpose of revising the text. It was then completely lost sight of for over twenty years until it was restored to its owner by Dr. Abraham. Later it was secured by Prof. Wagner in Marburg, who in turn passed it on to the Royal Library in Berlin. The contents of *C* include the Suites in D minor, C minor, B minor, A minor, the second E flat major Suite, and finally the fourth of the French Suites—i.e. the first Suite in E flat major. The works were written consecutively; only the second Allemande of the second E flat Suite was pasted in later, and the Minuet of the first E flat Suite is of earlier date. One's doubts are awakened by the numerous corrections, some of them made by erasure. The last lines of the Allemande and Courante from the C minor Suite actually appear on strips of paper that were pasted in subsequently. The extent to which these facts affect the authenticity of *C* may be determined by a comparison with *D*.

The *D* collection of manuscripts is of decisive significance in considering all important critical problems. Heinrich Nicolaus Gerber made these copies during the period of his study with Bach. Before me lie the copies of the French Suites (including the supplement), four English Suites, the Inventions and Symphonies, the beginning of the Well-Tempered Clavichord and several other items.

According to the testimony of his son, the lexicographer, Gerber went to Leipzig in May 1724 and became a pupil of Bach half a year later. After two years of study he returned to his home. During the period of his work with Bach he studied the Inventions, many of the Suites, the Well Tempered Clavichord, finally—thorough-bass. The manuscripts in my possession appear approximately in the above sequence; they belong, in all probability, to the year 1725.

The following succession of the French Suites in Gerber seems to me to be more or less haphazard: 1) D minor, 2) A minor, 3) the second E flat major Suite, 4) B minor, 5) C minor, 6) the first E flat major Suite, 7) missing, 8) G major. The title is merely: "Suite pour le Clavecin." It is uncertain just which Suite was intended as #7. It may, perhaps, have been the one in E minor.

Of the English Suites, the Gerber manuscripts contain the ones in A major, G minor, E minor and D minor. The particular value of these copies lies not only in the care and fidelity of the execution of the manuscripts, but also in the fact that they were made during the time of Gerber's actual work with Bach—for purposes of study.

E is a good old manuscript of the C minor Suite. Many of the variants are similar to *B*. It is not particularly authoritative.

F is a copy of the first E flat Suite in very peculiar form. It contains a Prelude, Allemande, Courante, Sarabande, Gavotte, then another untraditional Gavotte of doubtful quality, finally an Aria. There is no Gigue. This manuscript is interesting in that it takes into consideration some of the doubtful corrections in *C*. But the whole form of the Suite is highly questionable.

In *G*, the Loure of the Fifth Suite is called a Bouree! The Allemande and Gigue are reversed, and written in a handwriting different from the rest of the manuscript. The authoritativeness of *G* is questionable.

H is a manuscript containing all six of the familiar French Suites. It is a good copy; but it is of importance only where the autographs are inadequate. The same can be said of the *J* manuscript. However, both *H* and *J* must be seriously considered in connection with any publication of the E major Suite.

K is a carefully prepared copy of the little E flat major Suite.

The first five French Suites were composed in 1722, the one in D minor may have been written even earlier. They were probably composed in the same succession as the sequence in which they have traditionally appeared in print. The autographs contain no preludes. In *D*, the E major Suite contains a Prelude; in *F*, the first E flat major Suite; in Peters, the A minor and E minor Suites—the latter also in *D*. The Minuets in the C minor and B minor Suites were written later.

Insofar as the English Suites are concerned, the province of criticism becomes a much easier field to traverse; for it is much simpler to trace the genesis of these works. The title, "English Suite," is an unimportant nickname. Forkel's explanation that these Suites were ordered by an eminent Englishman is supported by *C;* but the inscription appearing in this manuscript—"fait pour les Anglais" was inscribed on the title-page in a strange handwriting. The true title should be: "Suite avec prélude," i.e. "Suite with a Prelude."

I have utilized the following manuscripts:

A. This is the autograph proper, belonging to Mr. Hauser in Karlsruhe. Spitta was not acquainted with this source. The ending of the first Suite appears in a strange handwriting.

B. The Gerber copies of the Suites in A major, G minor, E minor and D minor. (Compare our discussion of the Gerber copies under *D* of the French Suites.)

C. A manuscript in the possession of Mrs. Mendelssohn in Berlin. It is complete up to the F major Suite. The latter contains the signature: Jean Chrétien Bach. There is no proof that it was really finished by the latter. However, the whole manuscript gains in importance because it had been the property of Johann Christian Bach.

D. A good, complete earlier copy—also belonging to Mrs. Mendelssohn.

E. No. 489 in the Amalien-library. Good and complete.

F. No. 50 in the Amalien-library. Somewhat later than *E;* equally complete and dependable.

G. No. 291 of the Royal Library in Berlin. This is a complete copy.

Fragments of the Suite collections appear in the following:

H. No. 56 in the Amalien-library.

J. No. 212 in the Royal Library in Berlin.

K. No. 218 in the Royal Library in Berlin.

L. This is a collection of five Preludes from the English Suites (the first is omitted). Property of Dr. W. Rust—inherited from the legacy of F. W. Rust.

There are no difficulties in presenting the text. The autograph is a careful "fair copy"; the Gerber manuscripts follow the autograph very literally, even to the inclusion of errors in script. If the authenticity of *A* needed any confirmation, it could certainly be supplied by *B*. I believe it is highly probable that *B* was copied directly from *A;* the proof of this lies in the similarity of many of the errata. It is only in relation to these errata that our sources from *C* to *L* become important. There are very few deviations in the form of the Suites. In *A*, the continuity of the Suites is sustained. If *B* is a direct copy of *A*, then we are justified in believing that all the English Suites (including those not appearing in Gerber) were completed by 1725. One can be just as certain of the continuity of the six Suites as one is of the construction of the individual Suites. In the English Suites we have a collection which Bach himself put together; in the French Suites we assume that his final intention is the familiar traditional selection of six Suites.

As a final note I should like to mention that I have not always taken into consideration the extremely detailed indication of ties and dots in the autographs. The ties appearing in heavier type are traditional. All the ornaments appearing in the text, including the quick appoggiaturas indicated by little apostrophes, are authentic.

Berlin, 1881.

DR. HANS BISCHOFF.

TABLE OF EMBELLISHMENTS

For the uninitiated performer the following indications will suffice—in reference to this volume.

1) Grace notes, like all other embellishments, enter ON the beat—not before it. Unless indicated otherwise, they should be executed quickly.

2) The trill (tr or ~~) generally begins on the auxiliary note. There is usually an after-beat, unless this is replaced by one or more indicated notes. The after-beat is unnecessary before a descending second. The symbol for the trill with an up-beat is ~~ or ~~. The trill starting on the lower note ~~  and the one starting on the upper note ~~  usually both end with an after-beat. The following symbols may also be used to indicate the same: ~~ and ~~ . The short trill ~  is usually tied to the upper second preceding. Its symbol frequently takes the place of ~~ and tr.

3) The mordent  or  often takes the tone a minor second lower as the auxiliary note, although the neighboring note is sometimes a major second lower. (Compare Türk, Ch. IV p. 61.)

4) The turn ~ placed over a note is executed , placed between two notes it is played 

In dotted rhythm, the turn proper ends on the dot 

5) The slurred note ~ is played 

6) Other embellishments are explained in the annotations.

DR. HANS BISCHOFF.

SIX FRENCH SUITES

and two suites in A minor and E♭ major

SUITE I.

D minor

ALLEMANDE.

Andantino. ♩ = 72.

1) Variant in *B*: 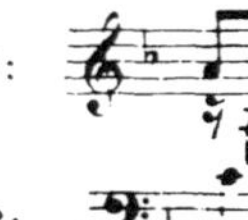 2) Variant in *C*: , compare measure 7. 3) Variant in *B*: , compare measure 5

4) Variant in *B*:

1) According to *C*, the middle voice is: 

SARABANDE.

Andante. ♩ = 76.

1) From this point on, the first Suite is also extant in *A*.

2) According to B.  , in conformity with the ending of the Courante.

3) According to Reinecke (Breitkopf & Haertel):  This is musically sound and thematically correct; but where is its origin?

MENUET I.
Moderato. ♩ = 108.
m.s.
cresc.
espressivo
dim.
crescendo
MENUET II.
grazioso
NB
N.B.

GIGUE.

Moderato. ♩= 100.

1)  in *B.*

2)  according to *B. A* contained the same version, but the B natural was subsequently crossed out. The B natural is missing in *C and D.*

N.B. The more precise notation of this figure would be:  but not 

Compare Page 27, note 5 in Bach's "Two and Three Part Inventions"—Kalmus edition.

1) D instead of C in *B*. 2) G instead of F in *B*. 3) *A* ends at this point.

SUITE II.

C minor

ALLEMANDE.

Andante. ♩= 69.

1) In *C*, the two eighth-notes on G are replaced (through erasure) by one quarter-note.

2) In *D* the apparent notation  is obviously incorrect!

3) From this point on, the correction in *C* is made on a piece of paper pasted over the original sheet.

COURANTE.

Allegro. 𝅗𝅥. = 60.

1) Variant in *D*. 

2) According to *B E H* and *J*: 

3) According to *D*: 

1) Bach was undecided concerning the B natural and E natural in these two respective measures. Yet it would seem that his final decision was to retain them.

2) In *D* there conspicuously appears a G flat instead of the G natural.

3) Our text is according to *C*, which contains the corrected version on pasted-over paper. The ensuing 15⅓ measures are replaced in *D* by the following:

In *A*, where only the second part of the Courante is preserved, one finds the following version of the same section:

According to *B H* and *J*:

The ending is the same as in *D* and *A*. The *E* is similar to *B H* and *J*, except that the notes marked with a + are a scalewise-third lower. (Compare *D*.)

SARABANDE. NB.

Andante. ♩= 72.

1) According to *A* and *D*: . 2) According to *B*:  3)  *E*. 4) B flat instead of C, an error in script in *D*.

5) According to *C* and *E*. In *C* there is an erasure. According to *H* and *J*: ; According to *A* and *D*: . In *B* there is a distorted version.

6) *B* breaks off at this point. 7) According to *E H* and *J*: 

N.B. The manuscripts contain a number of slurs in the upper voice; however, this is not done consistently enough to warrant their retention.

AIR.

Allegretto. ♩= 80.

1) In *A*, this D appears through correction as an A natural contrary to later manuscripts.

2) A flat according to *A D H J* and the first notation in *C*. Subsequently the A flat was changed to a G in *C*—in keeping with the version in *E*.

3) The traditional substitution of E natural for E flat and of B natural for B flat was doubtless due to errors in script.

4) A flat, according to *H* and *J*.

MENUET.

Moderato. ♩ = 120.

1) The second ending is according to *D*. 2) According to *E*:  3)  according to *E*.

4) G instead of C in *D* through an error in script.

N.B. The ties are authenticated by the manuscripts.

GIGUE.

Allegro. ♩. = 96.

1) *A* breaks off at this point.

2) Error in 'script in *D*: D instead of E flat.

3) Subsequent correction in *D*:

4) B flat instead of C in *E* and *H*.

1) Error in script in *D*: C instead of D.

2) According to *E*: 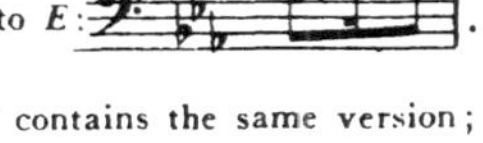 .

3) *C* contains the same version; subsequent correction: . In *E*:

SUITE III.

B minor

ALLEMANDE.

Moderato. ♩ = 92.

1) *A* also contains the B; on first glance the note might also have been a G. The edition of the "Bach-Gesellschaft" seems to have erred in this respect.

2) This F sharp was subsequently added in *C* and was thence carried over into *D*.

3, 4) The notes B and A sharp appear to be a later correction in *C*. *A* contains F sharp both times; yet even in this version the author seems to be undecided concerning this figure.

5) *C* contains C sharp in place of B through an error in script.

COURANTE.

Allegro. 𝅗𝅥. = 60.

1) The written grace-note appears only in *C.*

SARABANDE.

Andante con moto. ♩ = 92.

espressivo

1) The version in *D* and *H* [music example] appeared originally in *C*.

2) Original version in *C*, similar to that in *A* *D* and *H*: [music example]

3) The long notes, which must be sustained, are not indicated in *D*; they do appear in *C*.

4) In *D* [music example]; this is merely a different manner of notation. 5) In *D*: ~ ⁓; this is missing in *C*.

6) D in *C*, obviously an error in script. In *H* the note is D sharp; in *D* it is C sharp.

N.B. These ties are traditional. I disregard certain other ties which are neither consistent nor necessary for precision of execution.

ANGLAISE.[3]

Allegro. 𝅗𝅥 = 92.

1) A later correction in *C* is: 2) Originally *C* contained the version-which appears later in *D* as well as in *H* and *J*:

3) As a rule this piece is erroneously named a Gavotte. 4) According to *D*: 5) The fragment of the Anglaise in *A* commences at this point.

6) According to *A H* and *J*: , likewise in *C* originally—subsequently altered in conformity with *D* and our text. 7) Originally *C* contained the version appearing in *A D* and in our text. The subsequent correction was: . Still later the original version was restored. 8) The B is a subsequent correction in *C*, replacing the D which appeared in *A* and *D*.

MENUET.

Allegro grazioso 𝅗𝅥. = 60.

TRIO.

1) In A H and J:  2) Through an error in script the B appears an octave higher in C. The lower B is justified by its appearance in A and the subsequent correction in D.

3) Variant in A H and J:  4) According to A H and J: 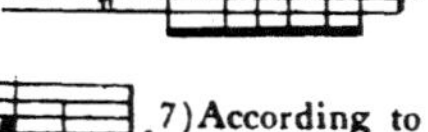. 5) Our text is based on A H and J. In C and D there appears the inferior reading 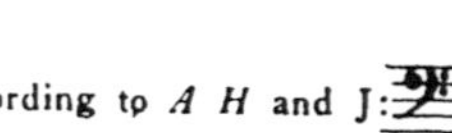 6) According to A H and J: . 7) According to A H and J:

8) According to A H and J: 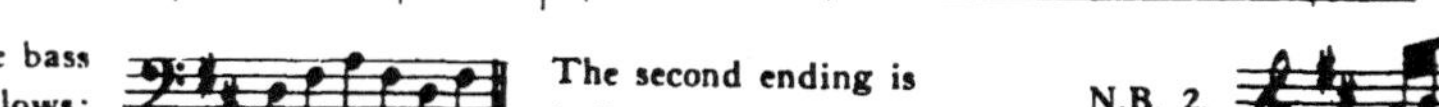

N.B. 1. According to C, the bass in the first ending is as follows:  The second ending is similar to our text.

N.B. 2.  or  similar to the way the figure is written out in measure 6.

Menuet da Capo.

GIGUE.

Vivace. ♩ = 80.

1) In *A C* and *D* there is no sharp before the second G. *H* and *J* contain the G sharp.

1) *C* contains D instead of B—an obvious error. 2) Later correction in *C*: *D* sharp instead of E. 3) Originally in *C*, in conformity with *A H* and *J*:

. The G was subsequently changed to A in *C*—this change was carried over into *D*. Its justification lies in the imitation.

SUITE IV[NB]

E♭ major

ALLEMANDE.

1)  in *A F H* and *J*; also originally in *D*. This was later altered in conformity with *C* and our text. 2) In *A* there is no natural sign before the A

3) C instead of B flat in *C* through an error in script. 4) Error in script in *C*: . 5) This natural sign before the A appears in *C F H* and *J*. 6) According to *F*: .

N.B. *C* contains many corrections of questionable authenticity. We indicate these with alphabetical symbols. The references which also contain the symbol ⌖ are to be found in *F* as well as in *C*. Some of these examples are interesting because of their melodic ornamentation, others contain various details of interest. The performer can make his own choice.

a) ⌖  b) Notes of longer value. c) ⌖ . d) G instead of B flat. flat. e) The following version also appears in *F*, except that the opening note is A flat instead of A natural:  f) Notes of longer value. g) ⌖ 

COURANTE.

Allegro. ♩= 120.

1) According to F:  2) This measure is omitted in F.

N.B. The traditional execution of this type of rhythm is:  The following is incorrect: 

SARABANDE.[NB]

Andante con espressione. ♩ = 76.

1) F instead of G in *C*, through an error in script. 2) The F is missing in *C* and *D*. It does appear, however, in *A F H* and *J*. 3) A flat instead of A natural in *A*—similarly in *H* and *J*. 4) In *A H* and *J*:  in place of .

N.B. Several slurs appear in the manuscript. However, the entire piece is supposed to be played legato.

h) ⊕  i) ⊕ An E flat is added above the F. k) ⊕ An A flat is added above the D flat. l) ⊕ The following is added:  m) ⊕ A G is added below the B flat. Moreover, longer values are given to the notes in *C*. Similarly in ***F***.

GAVOTTE. NB 1.

Vivace. 𝅗𝅥 = 80.

MENUETT. NB 2.

Allegretto. ♩ = 120.

1) F sharp in *A*. In *C*, the F sharp was later inscribed over the A; *F* and *H* both contain the F sharp.
2) G instead of B flat in *F*.

N.B.1. The ties in heavier type are authentic.

N.B.2. This piece is derived from *C*, to which it was subsequently added. Compare the discussion in the Preface dealing with the subsequent addition of some of the Minuet movements.

N.B.3. In the repetition, the left hand should obviously play only 

n) ⊕  . At + there is a G instead of an A flat in *F*.

o) ⊕ 

AIR.

Moderato. ♩ = 104.

1) The D is according to *A* and *D;* the E flat in *C* is erroneous.
2) A flat in *C D* and *F*; A natural in *A H* and *J*; compare the similar section in the second part of this piece.
3) A flat instead of A natural in *C F* and *J*. 4) 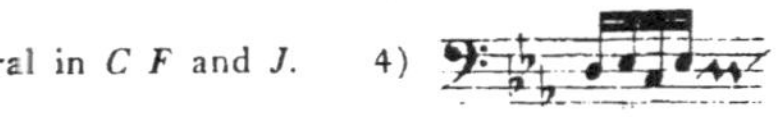 in *F*.
5) E flat through subsequent correction in *C*, which at first contained the D which is also to be found in the *A* and *D* versions.
6) According to *C* and *D*. In *A*, the E flat and D appear an octave lower; similarly in *F H* and *J*.

GIGUE.

Vivace. ♩. = 112

1) A natural in place of A flat in *A*.

N.B. The trill extends only throughout this measure.

1) According to the correction in *C*; elsewhere one finds an E flat instead of the C. 2) *A* originally contained:

Later the right hand was altered in conformity with our text; subsequently the bass was changed as follows:

N.B. The trill extends only throughout this measure:

p)

q)

SUITE V.

G major

ALLEMANDE. N.B.

Allegretto. ♩= 96.

1) The B is omitted in *G* and *H*. 2) The E is omitted in *H* and *J*. 3) According to *H*: 

4) B instead of C in *G*. 5)  in *D*.

N.B. The ornaments in small type appear in *D*; some of them are also to be found in *H* and *J*. The Editor advises that the trills be played.

COURANTE.

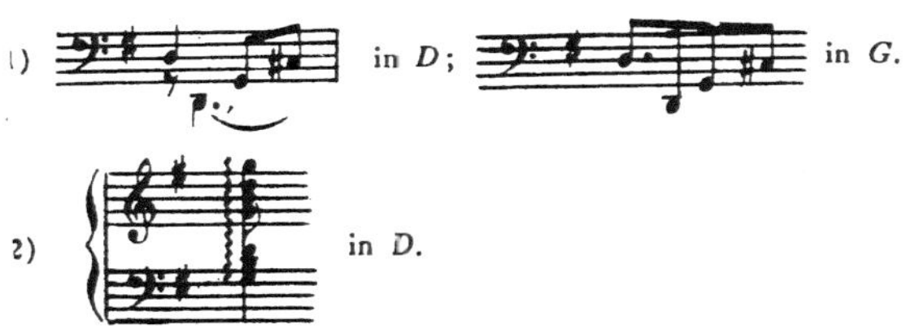

SARABANDE.[N.B.]

Andante con moto. ♩ = 88.

1) C sharp according to *H* and *J*.

2)  in *J*. 3)  in *D*.

N.B. The ties are authentic. I am retaining them as an illustration of the inadequacy of the old method of notation. Legato playing is predominant in this movement.

1)  D.

2)  in *H*.

3) A instead of B, in *H* and *J*.

4) The following two measures are replaced by this variant in *D*:

This version also appears in the oldest Hoffmeister-Kuhnel printing, where several ties are also to be found in the triplet section.

GAVOTTE.

Allegro 𝅗𝅥 = 80.

BOURRÉE.

Allegro. 𝅗𝅥 = 96.

1)  in *D*.

2) 𝆖 is supposed to be played though it is missing in *A*.

LOURE. 4)

Moderato. ♩ = 120.

1) Our text is according to *A H* and *J*. *D* contains:  This version also appears in the oldest printing.

2)  in *H* and *J*. 3)  in *D*.

4) The Loure appears in *A*, but not in *D*. This piece is inaccurately named Bourree #2 both in *G*, in the Bach-Gesellschaft edition and elsewhere.

5) The F sharp is missing in *G*. 6) In *G*, the soprano has C, the middle-voice has A. 7) In *G*, the middle C and the G in the left hand are missing.

GIGUE.

Presto. ♪. = 132.

1) According to D, and G. In A H and J: . Similar rhythmic deviations of no vital consequence are to be found elsewhere.

2) According to G: . 3) In H and J, A instead of F sharp through an error in script. 4) In G the continuation of the Gigue appears three pages earlier.

1) D instead of E in *D*. 2) In *D* and *G*: [musical example]. In *H* and *J*: [musical example]. 3) In *D* and *G*: [musical example].

4) The A and the B alluded to in this reference are both written a note higher in *D* and *C*. 5) The middle voice in *G* is: [musical example]

SUITE VI.[1)]

E major

ALLEMANDE.[NB]

Allegretto vivace. ♩ = 104.

1) In *D*, this Suite opens with the ninth Prelude from Vol. 1 of the Well-Tempered Clavichord; the little Menuett appears at the close of the Suite.

2) D instead of D sharp in *H*. 3) B natural instead of B sharp, according to *D*.

N.B. The figure  has a tie over the first four sixteenth notes. This often reappears in the transpositions of the figure. One also finds several other ties.

1) D sharp instead of B, in *H* and *J*.

SARABANDE.

Andante. ♩= 76.

1) In *H* and *J*:    2) In *H* and *J*: 

3) According to *D*: E instead of F sharp.

GAVOTTE.

Allegro ma non troppo. 𝅗𝅥 = 80.

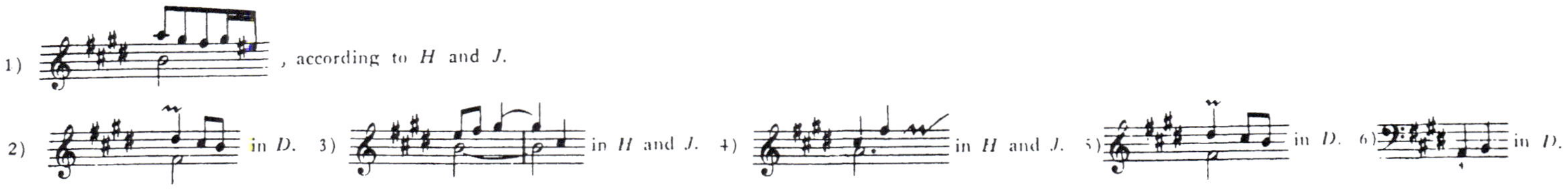

1) , according to *H* and *J*.

2) in *D*. 3) in *H* and *J*. 4) in *H* and *J*. 5) in *D*. 6) in *D*.

POLONAISE.

Allegretto. ♩ = 100.

MENUET. N.B.2.

Moderato. ♩ = 120.

1)  in *H* and *J*. 2)  in *D*; there is a distorted version in *J*.

N.B.1. In *H* and *J* one occasionally finds the indication tr in places where only a simple mordent is called for.

N.B.2. The ties given here are authenticated by the manuscripts. I have omitted several others which were only too self-evident.

BOURRÉE.

Molto Allegro. 𝅗𝅥 = 100.

1) The C sharp instead of E is presumably an error in script in *D*.

GIGUE.

Allegro. ♩. = 92.

1) F sharp instead of E sharp in *D*. 2) *D* instead of A in *H* and *J*.

SUITE POUR LE CLAVECIN №

Suite in A minor

di Joh. Seb. Bach.

ALLEMANDE.

Moderato. ♩ = 84.

1) In *C* there is an erroneous tie binding the two C's in the soprano.

2) According to *D*:

N.B. The ornaments appearing in lighter type are not authenticated by both *C* and *D*; most of them are derived from *D*.

COURANTE.

1) This figure always appears in *C* in the illogical rhythmic pattern of ♩. ♪♬

2) In *D*, this G is erroneously written as an A.

3) This is correct in *D*. In *C*, the C is erroneously written as an E.

SARABANDE SIMPLE.

Andante. ♩ = 76.

SARABANDE DOUBLE.

1) A instead of G, in *D*.

2) The version of the ornament in the manuscript is unquestionably erroneous.

3) In conformity with the previous measure, this beat could read:  It is quite possible that *C* and *D* contain a similar error in script.

1) E instead of F in *C*. It is quite likely that the same error in script appeared in *D* originally.

2) The sharp sign was omitted in *C*.

N.B. The repetition of the final four measures is absolutely necessary. The double version of the final measure given under 1. | 2. is definitely based on the necessity of this repetition. Whoever wishes to repeat the entire second section of the piece must, even the first time, use the A minor cadence given in the second ending.

GIGUE.

Allegro. ♩. = 92.

1) A in *C*, G in *D*. Compare the same figure two measures earlier.

p
cresc.
f
m.s.
p
sf
p
cresc.
f
Fine.

SUITE POUR LE CLAVECIN

Suite in E♭ major

ALLEMANDE.[NB]

Allegretto. ♩ = 84.

di Joh. Seb. Bach.

1)  in *K*. 2)  in *K*, without the two natural signs.

N.B. In the Allemande, ties are frequently to be found over the groups of four sixteenth notes, particularly on the first and third beats.

1) B flat instead of A flat, in *C*. 2)  subsequent correction in *K*.

3) The D flat appears in *K* as a subsequent correction of the otherwise traditional F. 4)  in *K*.

5) In *D* and *K* the final notes are sustained.

ALLEMANDE.[NB]

1) D flat instead of C flat in *C*. This is probably an error in script. Our text not only offers the prevailing motive with its precise intervals, but also retains the same harmonic sequence which appears a whole-step higher, with the voices inverted, in the second measure preceding. Our version, moreover, avoids one of the two cross-relations.

2) In *C*, there is a flat before the high C. This is presumably an oversight.

N.B. The second Allemande (a variation of the first Allemande, and presumably meant to be performed either instead of the first, or in place of its repetition) **appears** only in *C*; it was doubtless pasted in, and was written at a time when Bach's handwriting manifested different idiosyncracies of style. Its authenticity seems to me **to be fairly certain in view of the boldness with which Bach wrote the piece. Compare the note to the Menuett in the other E flat Major Suite, which shows similar idiosyncracies in the handwriting.**

mf
cresc.
f
p
marc.
crescendo
f

COURANTE.[NB]

Allegro. ♩ = 160.

1) The arpeggio signs appear in *D*.

2) Subsequent correction in *C*:

This may be authentic. In any event, it sounds satisfactory. Note the absence of the natural sign at +!

3) According to *C*, this apparently sometimes appears: ⁓ ≈. 4) In *K*, there appears the correction: B flat instead of C.

5) E flat according to *K*. In *C* and *D* there appears a D flat. This is less satisfactory—in view of the subsequent measure.

N.B. In *K* the Courante appears after the Sarabande.

SARABANDE.

Andante. ♩ = 72.

1) The A is tied, according to a later correction in *C*. 2) D instead of C in *D* and *C*. 3) A flat instead of G in *K*. 4) Two D's instead of the two G's in *K*!

5) *K*. 6) Subsequent correction in *C*:

BOURRÉE.

Allegro. 𝅗𝅥 = 96.

1) F instead of E flat in *K*; this is perhaps preferable—in view of the sequential figure appearing two measures later. 2) A subsequent correction in *C*: F instead of A.

3)  in *K*. 4) In *D* and *K* there is no natural sign. 5) B flat instead of A flat in *C*.

MENUET 1. (ALTERN.)

Allegro. ♩ = 126.

MENUET 2. TRIO.

1) F instead of E flat in *K*. 2) Subsequent alterations in *C*: 

3) According to *D* and *K*. In *C* there is a D in place of the B flat.

4) In *C* and *D* there is a natural sign before the A!!

Kalmus